Love, faith and suicide

Flor Del Monte

Love, faith and suicide

A personal experience

Santo Domingo, Dominican Republic,
2021

Love, faith and suicide.
A personal experience

Flor Del Monte

2021

Content

Dedication / 9

Acknowledgments / 11

Foreword / 13

Suicide / 17

Preface / 21

Introduction / 23

Day 1 / 29

Day 2 / 37

Day 3 / 41

The seventh day / 45

Days without truce / 49

Go ahead / 53

Reflection / 73

Epilogue / 75

Dedication

To my two children, who since their arrival in my life have been my source of inspiration, the engine that drives me to continue, the most precious gifts that God gave me, those who taught me not to give up and motivate me to keep going.

To my mother, for teaching me to be a tireless warrior with her example and perseverance, with her I learned how to fight for what you want.

Acknowledgments

To Pedro, my late husband, a wonderful human being, a good companion and an excellent father who, during his life's journey, always placed love for his family and humility in his treatment of others above all else, qualities that made him an exemplary man.

To Pedro Alejandro and Miguel Octavio, whom I admire for the courage and resilience with which they faced the loss of their father and for the trust they placed in me.

To my parents, for their unconditional support.

To Eddy, for supporting me in raising my children and for his loyalty during all these years.

To my dog Laika, my soul mate, my eternal companion and confidant.

And to each and every one of you who were there for us, in those hard and difficult moments of our lives.

But, above all, I thank with all my heart, the one who gave me the greatest support to continue, who supported me at all times and welcomed me with his warm love without abandoning me for a single day.

To you, my GOD, because without your presence, love and care I would not have made it.

«I can do everything through Christ, who strengthens me! »

Philippians 4:13

Foreword

Felix Maria Delmonte

For me it is an honor and a privilege to have been chosen by the author to write the foreword to this book, because I believe that this book is, in itself, a sapiential experience, a unique story of faith and an inspiring work that can help many people to heal after being exposed to the suicide of a loved one.

Suicide, according to the world health organization, is «Any self-inflicted human act, performed with the implicit or explicit intent to die». Suicide and suicide attempts are not considered a mental disorder or illness per se, nor a mere reaction to situations of discomfort and distress. They are complex acts based on multiple biological, psychological and social factors (https//sprc.org).

My sister, the author of this book, whom I have known well since her childhood, explains in a simple way the whole process of a shocking event that transformed her life: the suicide of her beloved husband Pedro.

Suicide, as poetically defined by our brother Ricardo in his poem "Suicide", is a bloody monologue, like an inescapable deep abyss, which has no liturgy or commandment, and which makes life an impossible.

Flor, the author of this book, and her beloved husband met on a trip to the mountains, climbing Duarte Peak, when she was barely 20 years old. Ten months later they married and lived together for 23 years, during which time they had two wonderful sons, Pedro Alejandro and Miguel Octavio.

Life seemed to smile at them, Flor was happy! Pedro was an exemplary father and an excellent companion. We never imagined that her marriage would end with the suicide of her lover.

All of us who had the opportunity to know Pedro remember him as an introverted, loving, humble and jovial person, who loved his wife and children, as well as all the other members of his family. Therefore, his suicide was like a sordid bell at four o'clock in the morning, for all of us who knew him intimately.

His family expressed that at first glance everything was fine with Pedro, so the news of his death shocked us all, but it was Flor who was shaken to the core of her being.

It is from this overwhelmingly traumatic experience that this book is born, which more than a book is a story of faith, which breaks with religious, moral and social archetypes about suicide and gives way to the knowledge of a God of love that does not fit in contemporary religious precepts, but yes in the inspired revelation of his word. (Joel 2:32) «And it will come to pass that everyone who calls on the name of the Lord will be saved...» «For in my distress I called on the Lord, and cried to my God; He heard my voice from his temple, and my cry reached his ears» (Samuel 22: 7).

Flor, we have seen you struggling against adversity, against despair and against giants. Now I know where your help came from... your help came from the LORD, who made the heavens and the earth. Those of us who know you saw the power of faith in action, the mercy of God and the redeeming grace of our Lord Jesus Christ guiding your steps and filling you with victories.

Thank you for writing this testimony of love, courage, hope and persistence. Your example of faith will impact thousands of lives that suffer from the loss of a loved one who suddenly ended their life here on earth.

Beloved reader, I know this book will inspire you and give you spiritual and practical tools to deal with feelings of anger, guilt and rejection.

It will also provide you with the communication strategies necessary to accept grief and the strength to emerge from a place of thick darkness into the marvelous light of a God of love who is able to reveal himself to all who call upon him with a genuine heart, for his heart's desire is to comfort us in all our troubles, so that we too may comfort those who are in any trouble, through the consolation with which we are comforted by God.

I promise you, the pages of this book will bring you ground, give you strength and transform you, just as my sister Flor was transformed. God's love, grace, mercy and peace stand out on every page of this book, which I am sure was inspired to inspire by the One who is the Wonderful, the Counselor, the Mighty God, the Eternal Father, the Prince of Peace.

Orlando, FL., October 2021

Suicide

Ricardo Delmonte

In that cavern so dark, there was a
mysterious riddle,
written by a monster in his madness,
to make men sorrowful.

Through that devilish labyrinth,
the souls dragged the chains,
on a paved floor of fire,
that increased the pain of sentences.

In there a second becomes eternal,
it is a biochemical and evil galaxy,
that tortures souls with its winter,
wanting to be saved by death.

There is blindness in the splendorous afternoon,
laughter hurts your reason,
there is deafness in the glorious music,
the flowers in retinas, like a punch.

Suicide is a bloody monologue,
like an inescapable deep abyss,
which has no liturgy or commandment,
and which makes life an impossible.

If you knew that there are people who love you,
if you knew that there is always a solution,
if you could with chemistry that hurts,
you could heal your heart.

Those who are wounded forever,
heal memories with love,
the affection remains as a reference,
of the loving God who was its author.

Santo Domingo, June 2021

Love, faith and suicide

A personal experience

Preface

This is where it all began...
23 years of traveling with the love of my life.

When I was already 20 years old, I was able to go on my first excursion to Duarte Peak with the university I was attending at the time. It was an exciting, fun and renewing trip.

In the group, out of almost 60 people traveling together, there were only six women and the rest were men.

Can you imagine that it was there that I met the man who would become my life partner?

When we returned from the trip, we all kept in touch and a few days later he asked me to be his girlfriend and unbelievably, without knowing him, I practically said yes. Ten months later we were already getting married. It was a union that lasted 23 years, resulting in two beautiful children.

I won't say it was a perfect life, because nothing on earth is perfect, but it was a good marriage and a nice family, because he was an exemplary father and an excellent partner.

After I got married, I never thought that my marriage would end with my husband's suicide; I always imagined being with my life partner until we were old, because I have always been a hopeless romantic, I believe in family, but, like everything in life, man proposes and God disposes.

But he was an extraordinary human being, with flaws like everyone else, however, his worst problem was not knowing how to handle himself when it came to economic problems.

I was always there to help and support him, but as usual in these cases, I, in my day-to-day effort, was not able to observe his state of mind more thoroughly at that moment and notice that, perhaps, something was not right.

The truth is that, between the economic problems we were facing at that time, the absorbing and demanding work I had, activities and other responsibilities with the children, the house... I didn't realize how his mood changed.

As in most suicide cases, Peter showed no visible signs that anything was affecting him. Communication at the time did not flow from him to the family, something that took me years to understand. Nevertheless, from the bottom of my heart there is only love for him and I hope that God has forgiven and accepted him, because in his short stay in this world he was a noble and good human being.

Introduction

The poem that begins this book was written by my brother Ricardo, at my request, to introduce you to the subject of suicide in a poetic way without making you feel the fear, shame or remorse that we have been taught about this subject.

I am convinced that the survival instinct is the intrinsic ability that all living beings have, and this implies overcoming aggressions or changes in the environment (external or internal), with the aim of staying alive and, therefore, preserving the species.

If you try to kill a cockroach it quickly runs away, but, even worse, if you try to kill the offspring of any that can procreate, you will have to face the fury of its mother or father, depending on the species.

This is an instinct that all living beings bring from the moment of our conception, we do not have to study or develop it because it is born with us.

Survival, eating, drinking, sexual relations, are instinctive feelings that nature has programmed in living beings to preserve the species.

Even so, suicide has also been part of man's history since its beginnings. Whatever its moral, religious, sentimental, social, mental or religious causes or the reason that leads an individual to immolate himself, it should not be treated as a reason for shame, as a negative influence or to believe that a family is out of God's grace because of this fact. The Bible shows evidence of suicides:

"When Abimelech was mortally wounded by a woman who threw a millstone on his head, he cried out to his armor-bearer to kill him so that his death would not be attributed to the woman. " (Judges 9:54)

"King Saul, mortally wounded, fell on his own sword to prevent the Philistines from mocking him." (1.ra Samuel 31:4)

"Saul's armor-bearer also took his own life."
(1.ra Samuel 31:5)

"Ahithophel hanged himself after Absalom, King David's son, failed to follow his advice."
(2.a Samuel 17:23)

*"Zimri set himself on fire after his rebellion
failed."* (1 Reyes 16:18)

...and let us not forget that Judas hanged himself after betraying Jesus.

*And Saul said to his armor-bearer, Draw thy
sword, and thrust me through with it, lest
these uncircumcised come and thrust me
through, and mock me. But his armorbearer
would not, for he was sore afraid. So Saul
took his sword and fell upon it.
When his armor-bearer saw that Saul was
dead, he also fell on his sword and died with
him. So Saul died that day, along with his
three sons, his armor-bearer, and all his men.*
(Samuel 31:4, 5, 6)

When I went through the loss of my husband and heard all kinds of religious, moral, social and other arguments about suicide, I began to look for information and read everything I could get my hands on about the subject, because I realized how many taboos, myths and ignorance there are about it.

I found a lot of information in dozens of documents, but the truth is that the only one that shed light for me was faith in God, knowing Him and understanding His mercy towards and for us strengthened me and showed me how His love could make me overcome, overcome and move forward in spite of everything I was going through, as well as forgive and accept what had happened.

Loving God, I never felt alone or unprotected, I allowed Him to work in my case in His way and at His pace. And you will witness as you read the book that He was always by my side.

With him, I learned to put my love for my husband before any feeling that came to my thoughts or my heart, to only remember the wonderful and happy moments lived by his side and thus keep that memory and image for my children.

Focused, at all times, on the love for my children, making them the engine to move forward and face the future without falling into desolation, depression or bitterness for everything that happened. And, finally, living one day at a time was how I was able to move forward and find myself, today, in an emotional and spiritual state as I had never achieved before.

This book is only a summary of everything I want to tell you, I hope it will help you, since my goal is that it becomes a support tool and generate inspiration to continue extending my experiences through other texts.

"The grieving process allows you to find for your loved one the place he or she deserves among the treasures of your heart. It is to remember him or her with tenderness and to feel that the time you shared with him or her was a great gift. It is to understand with your heart in your hand that love does not end with death".

Jorge Bucay

Day 1

It was the middle of summer, a Monday, July 14, 2008. My oldest son had graduated from high school just a few days before and was on vacation at home, while my youngest son was attending a summer program offered by an international chain restaurant. I was at work and Pedro, my husband, was at work early in the morning with the driver running personal errands.

When we returned to the house, around eleven o'clock in the morning, Pedro asked Isabel, the lady who was helping us and cooking at the time, about our children, and she answered him:

-One is sleeping in his room and the little one is in camp.

As was his custom, Pedro set out to taste the food before it was served and then climbed the stairs to the third floor, where his office was located.

My eldest son was still asleep in his room when a few minutes later, both Isabel and Eddy, the driver, heard a gunshot and thought it was inside the house. The latter rushed upstairs to Pedro's office to make sure everything was all right. When he reached the third floor, he did not find him, checked the area and when he tried to open the office bathroom door he could not because it was locked from the inside.

At that moment, he sensed that something serious had happened and began to call him without getting an answer. Then he shouted loudly to the lady to wake up Pedro Alejandro so that he would go upstairs, who once he went upstairs, knocked and knocked on the bathroom door without getting any answer either. That was when he decided to climb up the back wall and look through the bathroom window to see if his father was there and God...! There he was, lying on the floor in a pool of blood, with the gun in his hand.

I can't imagine how much pain in that heart and everything that went through the head of a young man of only 18 years of age, just turned. My son's first reaction was to call me and say, –Mommy, you have to come quickly. I, who was with some clients at the time, told him: -I can't right now, but what's wrong? - And he, with no other alternative, had to tell me: -Come mommy, please, daddy shot himself.

Without saying a word, I got up from my desk, took my car and went to look for my vehicle. Everything became dark, silent, my mind could only think of my son, I answered the phone, –Call the police, I'm on my way.

I crossed back and forth several times on a busy avenue where my office was located, I couldn't find my vehicle, but I didn't remember that my husband had dropped me off at work that day and was using my vehicle.

I heard nothing, I just cried and begged God help my son! In that state of desperation I was able to make a call to my older brother, who lived near us, to come to the house while I arrived.

When Ricardo my brother arrived, he managed to kick down the bathroom door, only to confirm what had happened and the state Pedro was in. There was nothing that could be done, the shot had been in the head.

The reader may be wondering, why did I only think of asking God for my son? Simply because I knew, deep inside me, that if something had happened it would not have a solution, my husband knew a lot about guns and if something he had decided to do it would be irreversible. In truth, at that moment nothing else came to my heart except the horror that my still teenage son was experiencing.

Still in the middle of the avenue, what I call a "Godsidence" happened, more than a coincidence. Pedro's best friend, who worked in a building near mine, went out to have lunch at his house and when I saw him I asked him to take me to mine, something very serious had just happened and on the way I explained it to him. He was my first support.

My brother immediately confirmed the situation and called the police. My son had not thought to do so, which is a very understandable reaction. When the police officers arrived, as per protocol, they tested for gunpowder all those present at the time of the event, including my son, because of the moment he was going through and I was not with him!

When I finally arrived at the house, the police were still there, but the first thing I did was to look for Pedro Alejandro, who was in my room with his older cousin and, when he saw me arrive, he threw himself into my arms and his first words, crying, were: -Mommy, how am I going to tell my brother? It was incredible and admirable to me how he instinctively embraced the responsibility of taking care of his younger brother. To reassure him, I replied: -That's not your responsibility, it's mine, so don't worry, I'll take care of it.

Quickly, the house was filled with the whole family, neighbors and friends, some united in pain and others carried away by the morbidity that situations like this entail and with which some human beings wrap themselves up.

While we were waiting for the medical examiner to proceed with the removal of the body, some family members interrupted the solemnity and pain of that moment, driven by the morbid curiosity I am referring to, and searched my husband's office. In his computer they found a letter he had left for his children and they had the imprudence to read it.

At that moment there was no room for recriminations and I only managed to demand to everyone present that when my youngest son arrived, there would be no loud cries or screams, he would have enough with the news he was going to receive without having a tragic circus waiting for him.

Maybe, because of the situation, I was very hard on people, I didn't discriminate between some and others, but all I had in my mind was to protect my children.

When Miguel Octavio arrived at the house he knew immediately, because of the number of people and the presence of the policemen, that something serious had happened. I took him to my room and together with his brother, I explained to him what had happened. He was incredulous that something like this was happening, we cried a lot and he wanted to go upstairs to see his father, but I did not allow it, because I was not going to expose him to such a cruel image that was not for him to bear. I didn't want that picture to be in his heart, it was enough that the older boy had to face it alone.

The medical examiner was late in arriving, Pedro's lifeless body was in his office until four o'clock in the afternoon, adding anguish and pain to everyone.

I was so dazed, all kinds of thoughts and feelings were running through my head, as if it were a fast-motion movie. In one of those moments, I approached his body and complained to him so much, questioning him: "Why did you leave, idiot? Didn't you know that you mattered more to us than anyone else? So much was my pain, so much was my despair, that I bordered on insult.

My father was there, together with other family members, and with his characteristic coldness and equanimity, he put his hand on my shoulder and said: – Don't worry, my daughter, you are not alone. I can say that at that moment I knew that I had been left alone with my two children. Incongruous, isn't it? Her words of encouragement, the company she gave me, made me feel all the discouragement and loneliness that would fill my life in the future.

After the odious process of lifting the body and transferring it to the funeral home was completed, I went with my brother to organize everything related to his funeral. At that moment, everything for me was like a horrible dream.

One day you wake up next to the person you love, with whom you have years of a shared life, and that same day you are at the funeral home preparing his burial. It's surreal, you feel like you are asleep and will soon wake up, but no, all you had to face was the cruel reality.

At the wake, both my children and I found ourselves strengthened, something sustained and encouraged us, an inner strength nourished us, but even so, it was one of the worst moments of the whole process.

Recklessness, and again morbidity, made everything more difficult. Many of the people who approached us, even family members, talked to us about what had happened with expressions like these: "What was going on between your parents that your dad committed suicide"; "Your dad was not responsible for doing that"; "People who commit suicide do not go to heaven, they must pray a lot" or "a responsible man would not have done that". There were those who were so ruthless as to make this comment: "chronicle of a death foretold", alluding to some events that had preceded the decision made by Pedro.

But I repeat, the three of us had a supernatural force that kept us serene and calm. In those moments I got to know human cruelty, that which makes someone act in a twisted, morbid, critical way, that which easily leads us to make wood from the fallen tree. Since then I knew that I was going to defend and protect my children above all things and I cried out to God at every moment so that He would not leave me alone, I would need His presence in my life, at all times.

*«So do not fear, because I am with you; do not
worry, because I am your God.*

*I will strengthen you and help you; I will uphold
you with my victorious right hand."*

(Isaiah 41:10)

Day 2

The next day, the funeral service was scheduled so that after noon the burial would take place.

It is a Christian custom to have a funeral mass before burial, so I decided to leave the funeral home to find the pastor of the church I was attending to ask him to celebrate the mass.

Upon entering the parish house and being in her presence, I made the request and explained to her what had happened, the words she said to me at that moment would be sent by God himself, because they marked my life forever: "Daughter, I am not going to give you any sermon about this, I am only going to advise you the following "Live one day at a time", only in this way and by God's hand you will be able to move forward.

She told me that his family had gone through the same thing with his younger brother, who had committed suicide in his own home. Her mother had found him in his room, and only by living one day at a time and with love and faith in God, could her mother overcome that terrible tragedy.

The information at that moment was so powerful, I thought to myself and said: -Wow! my pain then is less than hers, because losing a child that way must be something terribly painful, and if she could overcome it, so can I, with God in front of me.

> That was one of the first signs that God
> was with me and would guide me to the
> extent that I gave him everything.

At the end of the funeral mass and before leaving for the cemetery, we had for the first time the opportunity to be alone, the three of us with our beloved father and husband, and to say goodbye.

At that moment, we each expressed to him, in our own way, how we felt about him, promising him that we would remain a family, and that we loved and would love him forever, because an instant would not erase or tarnish all that he had given us in life.

Together with all those who accompanied us, we started our way to the cemetery, following the hearse. How many painful, loving and sad feelings and thoughts flooded our hearts!

The silence was absolute, it is one of those moments in which the reality of what you are living hits you to the bone and the pain is so great that you simply have no way to defend yourself. At that moment, you just give yourself...

Neither of us wanted to show weakness, but just by looking at each other we knew what each of us was feeling.

Knowing that there is no return to see the lost person again is one of the most difficult feelings of detachment to handle, you are in limbo and just follow the pre-written script for these cases.

At the end of the funeral and thanking everyone who accompanied us, with my words I wanted to express that our family is still intact, that a member was physically missing, but that this one, from that moment on, was more present than ever, because he will always remain in our hearts. I wanted everyone to understand that we loved that person no matter what had happened.

When you get home, after this process, there is little you will remember; it is simply an act that begins and ends. From there, when only the memories, memories and thoughts generated by what has been lived remain, it is when your loved one begins to accompany you forever.

After his burial, the days passed and we did not know what to talk about. We did not sleep, in the house there was a painful and at the same time precious silence, because we felt the respect and warmth.

"In my distress I called upon the LORD, I cried unto my God;

He heard my voice out of his temple, and my cry came into his ears".

(Samuel 22:7)

Day 3

Our families are very Catholic and have the tradition of celebrating a novena for the deceased, this is dedicating and attending a daily mass for nine days.

In my eagerness to protect my children, I decided that I would not subject them to nine days of torture. I didn't mind being judged and yes, it was nine days of torture, just as it sounds, that would be spent all listening to the same litanies we had to endure during the funeral and burial. I only celebrated one mass, three days after the burial.

As head of the family, it was my turn to say a few words at the end of the service and I wanted to write them down, but everyone who knows me knows that I do not like to speak in public and that I hate to feel the center of attention, besides I suffer from stage fright, which added to all the pain and sorrow of the moment, did not allow me to write anything to read.

Nervous and desperate because I had to prove to my children that I could stand up for myself, I decided the night before to pray and ask God to speak through me, because he more than anyone else knew what my heart was feeling and wanted to express at that moment.

When the day of the mass arrived, the church was full with all our family and friends and, surprisingly, at the end, in spite of all the stage fright that invaded me, the pain that squeezed my heart and the pain I saw in my children, which knotted my throat, I was able to stand up and say the words of thanksgiving.

What I did at that moment surprised even me, because I was able to express and thank with my heart, **but I swear that each of the words that came out of my mouth that day were one more blessing received, confirming that God was accompanying me at all times.**

With all the emotional charge of an extremely emotional moment, with all the mixed feelings, the frustrations and the anger I felt when listening to some conversations, when we got home, I immediately had to, with the excuse of taking a bath, go into the shower so I could cry and unburden myself (yes, that's what I did for a long time, I cried while taking a bath, so the guys wouldn't find out, or at least that's what I thought. It was easier to tell them I got soap in my eyes).

At the same time, I thanked God for having calmed me down and put the right words in my mouth for that moment, for having given me the serenity to handle the whole situation without getting upset and not allowing myself to be turned into the instrument of human morbidity.

At the end of that day, my children and I could finally begin to manage, just us, our grief, supporting each other, crying freely, talking about it and beginning to decide how we wanted to go about this experience.

We decided to seek professional help and attend grief counseling; we also agreed to continue with everything we had planned for our lives up to that point: college, school, jobs, for example.

People should understand that for cases like this, the best company is in silence and that this company should be for short periods of time, because being alone is also very important to be able to organize your feelings and the decisions to be made.

The curiosity of the human being, sometimes unhealthy, of wanting to know what happened, we must learn to control it, out of respect and education.

I began a period of daily conversation with God, I asked Him tirelessly for the spiritual health of my children so that He would accompany them throughout their journey, because from that moment on He was their only father.

"For God has not given us a spirit of fear, but of power, of love, and of a sound mind."
(Timothy 1:7)

The seventh day

The following Sunday, just after my husband's death, I woke up with the desire to go to mass again, something told me to go to church. It was early, I left the children sleeping in the house and went out to see if I could find any mass, but all the morning masses had already passed.

When I arrived at my parish, I asked a lady who was leaving mass that day what time the next mass would be and she answered: "There is no mass until seven o'clock at night, but today there is a healing mass at three o'clock in the afternoon and that is yours.

I was a bit surprised. Why did this lady tell me that this was mine? Was my pain so obvious? Apparently yes, I had a haggard face and dark circles under my eyes from not sleeping, but it was strange that she told me that. I returned home and after lunch I asked my children -who were in the older one's room trying to fix a very old radio, work that their father had started and wanted to finish-, if they wanted to accompany me to a healing mass and they both said no, they were exhausted by everything that had happened, but I insisted again because I really did not want to go alone. The younger one ended up agreeing.

We went to the church and once there, seated to begin the mass, they closed the doors, scattered incense and the priest began to pray and call for the presence of the Holy Spirit to begin the healing. He asked everyone present to close their eyes; my son and I held hands and did so.

The following seconds I felt a hand, different from Miguel Octavio's, grabbing mine. As we were with our heads bowed in recollection, I wanted to confirm who was holding me, I opened my eyes a little and began to see a pair of fisherman's sandals, looking up little by little I observed a white tunic tied with a cord at the waist and when I saw his face, great was my surprise..., still remembering it, my eyes fill with tears and a unique sensation invades me.

I can assure you that the one who was holding my hand was Jesus himself. He asked me to take him to my house; suddenly we were already there and I opened the door; as we entered, he stopped in front of the family photo placed in the hall. He looked at me with merciful and loving eyes, smiled and went upstairs to the room of my eldest son who remained in the same position as I had left him, sitting on his bed. There I could see how Jesus placed his hands on his head and the whole room lit up, with a glowing and warm light at the same time. Then we returned to the church.

When I consciously opened my eyes again, both my youngest son and I were still holding hands, crying, because we were overcome by an emotion of pain, but at the same time of consolation.

From that moment on, there was no doubt in my mind: **my children and I would be fine.** Resilience took hold of me, I felt protected and blessed for everything that awaited me from that moment on.

Yes, I know, there are many doubts and comments. Some will say

–You made that up, who will she believe for Jesus to approach her?–, –That was a product of stress and so on. Well, I'll tell you, whatever happened, believe me that the strength that this experience gave me helped me get ahead and helped me raise my children.

I myself was confused, I did not dare to tell anyone what I had experienced, I knew the reactions that people could have and at that moment I was not ready to bear even a little more pressure.

The following week I went to talk to my pastor about my experience and I loved his wise words:

"well, if it was true and that only you and God know, you have been blessed and if it was a figment of your imagination for all you have been through, I am glad your imagination has given you that tool to move forward. One way or the other, both are blessings."

So, no matter what others think, I know what I experienced and how it marked me forever.

The only thing I am certain of is that at all times I cried out to God and never claimed anything from Him, to give Him the power to resolve and arrange things as best suited my children and me.

Days without truce

The following days, weeks and months I faced embargoes, threats, lawsuits, as a result of all the debts that Pedro had incurred, to finish the construction that had been entrusted to him as a contractor engineer, for which we were going through very difficult economic times, due to defaults in the payment of the contracting party.Everything I owned up to that moment and everything I was able to get in loans, from the sale of furniture, clothes and valuables, was used to fulfill the inherited commitments and to get some peace of mind.

For years I continued and faced a legal claim for the request of payment of the aforementioned work, battling judicially against one of the most powerful consortiums of that time, which I was able to do with the efficient support of a lawyer friend.

While that was happening, I continued working full time to make my children see that we were moving forward and to be an example to them. It was very important for them to understand how to face and handle problems in order to solve them and continue living without bitterness or reproaches of any kind. That life became my day to day and without any respite.

They were years of intense stress, with a force that I myself did not understand, but I knew where it came from.

"In the face of all problems we are more than conquerors through him who loves us."
(Romans 8:37)

Months after that July 14, we received the notice that we were granted the U.S. residency visa requested by my mother. Even Pedro's visa arrived and had to be returned.

At the time I was surprised at the speed with which the process was completed, and now, looking back, I consider that it was nothing more than the safe-conduct that God sent so that my children could have the opportunity to start a new life, where they would not be haunted by the shadow of human evil that does not allow others to rise up in the face of their difficulties. First my oldest son emigrated and then my youngest, where they got scholarships and federal aid for their studies. I was left all alone and still with many problems to solve.

The court case was long and very stressful; after some time it went to arbitration, a process by which the dispute is submitted, with the agreement of the parties, to an arbitrator or tribunal that issues a decision on the dispute and whose compliance is binding on the parties.

Everyone told me that I would not win the case, always with arguments loaded with a lot of negativity, but especially because the other side was represented by very powerful lawyers.

I told everyone, including my lawyer when I sometimes doubted: **I am going to win this case!** At all times I was sure, I never doubted. Even with a verdict in my favor, when the time came to execute the sentence, I had to negotiate the amount requested, because I was up against a very powerful economic sector. It didn't matter if I received less, **I win!!**

The truth is that, although some may not believe it, I was not bothered by the amount recovered in the least, because I was not litigating for the money (although I needed it to get out of trouble), I had done it because I wanted to teach my children how to deal with problems.

That they could see that I did not give up, it gave them the assurance that they could count on me for everything and that I was not the fragile woman who became a widow and inspired pity, but that, on the contrary, I am a warrior with God's grasp, ready to do everything for them and also to redeem and clear her father's name.

I knew who was beside me, and that left no room for doubt, nor did it allow fear in me.

"Learn to do good!
Seek justice and rebuke the oppressor!
Advocate for the fatherless and
defend the widow!".
(Isaías 1:17)

Although we won the case in court, it was far from solving the economic problems I was facing. I received less money than requested because of the negotiation and being alone, with my children in the United States, I found myself in the need to sell the house, because it was the only thing that could provide enough funds to pay off the debts and be able, once and for all, to have some peace and tranquility.

At all times my children agreed and I will always be grateful to them for thinking of my welfare and trusting me.

Three years had passed and it was then that I was able to start from scratch and get organized. I had my job, it would only be a matter of time, perseverance, endurance and faith to recover some of what I had lost. The most important thing is that none of the three of us lost the most essential thing in life: love and support for each other as a family.

Focused on moving forward, we take advantage of experience to become stronger, more intelligent, more cautious, more resilient, more human, more humble, and thus grow more within ourselves. For me, in particular, to confirm the existence and presence of God in my life.

"Whoever confesses that Jesus is the Son of God, God abides in him, and he in God."
(John 4:15)

Go ahead

I want to share with you, the events that I understand helped us to move forward, situations that took place as a family before and after, and that we endured to overcome.

It is not a psychological guide or anything like that, they are experiences and decisions that gave me and my children the tools to continue.

I will only summarize them, because they worked for us. It is not the same when someone who has not gone through what you are going through gives you advice or consoles you, as it is to listen to, in this case to read, advice and experiences from someone who has gone through and overcome the same tragedy.

However, reading books about suicide and grief also helps a lot. I read everything that was recommended to me and did a lot of research on the subject.

Receiving therapy from a psychologist, a specialist in grief, is also of great help; however, what allows you to overcome everything is the attitude with which you face what happened. No one can help those who do not want to be helped.

Of all the above, the most important thing is to fix your support on the one who will always be there for you -

-without any kind of interest and without any demands-, that is the real key, and only **God** can offer you that.

"Be strong and of good courage; fear ye not, neither be afraid of them: for the LORD thy God is he that goeth with thee; he will not fail thee, nor forsake thee.

And the LORD goes before you; He will be with you, He will not leave you, nor forsake you; do not be afraid nor be dismayed."

(Deuteronomy 31:6-8)

✳

Family communication

The communication we had always developed with our children, including them and keeping them informed of everything that happened at home, between us, in our jobs and in our surroundings, helped them understand a little of why their father made that decision. In our house there were never any secrets or taboos when it came to talking.

My husband and I were of the opinion that the children are part of the house and the family, therefore, they have the right to be aware of everything that happens in them; of course, always with the level of depth according to the age of the children, who should always be aware of the situations that their parents are going through.

Maybe many people think it shouldn't be that way, but it worked well for us. It helped my children to learn what we did well and not so well, so they kept their feet on the ground, so they wouldn't make the same mistakes. On the other hand, being aware of all the problems their dad was facing allowed them to not be left with feelings of guilt or dislike for him. It also allowed us, after the bereavement, to talk to each other about how we felt about what had happened.

All members of the family should be aware of what is going on in the home with each of its members, whether they have health, behavioral, financial, legal or any other problems. In this way, there will be no surprises when an unexpected event occurs.

"Listen, my son, to the discipline of your father,
and do not forsake the teaching of your
mother."
(Proverbs 1:8)

❊ ❊

Avoid feelings of anger,
guilt and rejection

There are many feelings that surface when we go through this type of mourning and it is one of the most difficult things to overcome. Why did he do it? What was going through his mind? Did he not care about us? Did he not love us?

Let's not get bogged down there. I know it is difficult, believe me, but you must try not to let those thoughts cloud your good memories of the lost person and let only what he contributed to your life matter. Remember only his virtues; it is not to praise what he did, but neither to dye black his entire journey through life. Do not let the pain cloud your hearts or your thoughts!

Within all the misfortune I had the "happiness" of, first, having the obligation to continue taking care of my children; second, a secure job, even when it was demanding and demanding, and third, having inherited my husband's financial problems.

I say it was fortunate that those urgencies and priorities took up all my time, because after the fact, when I could think clearly, there was so much that had happened that I only had the option of moving on. There was no room for much else, let alone getting depressed.

It is not that there were not moments of sadness, crying and immense loneliness, but I was so busy and full of urgent and vital tasks, that these periods were quite short, not giving me the chance to fall into deep crises.

It is important to observe if you feel anxiety, difficulty thinking, if you are agitated, irritable, tense, if you have a headache, trembling, a feeling that something bad is going to happen, angry outbursts or difficulty sleeping, because these are symptoms that you should take care of immediately.

If you don't, both your physical and mental health will be seriously affected. If you wear yourself out, your body will suffer, your social and communication skills will diminish, causing many people to distance themselves from you, and you will lose bonds that could help you in the healing process.

If you allow those feelings to take over, it will be very difficult for you to get up and move on.

Talk to God, unburden yourself to Him, tell Him what you are feeling; then be silent so that you can listen to His answers.

Try to see the sun when you wake up and the stars when you go to bed and be grateful for everything you have experienced with the person you lost. You will see how you begin to find peace and little by little balance.

"Remove from you all bitterness, anger, wrath,
shouting and slander, and all malice."
(Ephesians 4:31)

❋ ❋ ❋

Why?

Searching for the cause of why the loved one commits suicide is no longer important. What done is done. You can't go back. Even if we found out why, this is not going to bring us back to the loved one and the response may leave us more hurt.

The physical loss is already emotionally exhausting enough to add to the wear and tear involved in the search for an explanation, which most of the time is known only to the person who committed the act and to God, no one else.

Block this questioning completely, both from your mind and from your heart, so that you do not get involved in the selfish intrigue of looking for a reason or motive for what happened.If you lost your family member in an accident or through illness, you would not look for causalities. With suicide it should be the same, it is a loss like any other; the way it happens should not make a difference in moving on. You miss and remember the one who leaves this world just the same, then,
why make mourning different?

Sometimes you will find a why left by the suicidal person to his family, but it will never be the real reason, because at that moment the suicidal person has an unusual or normal way of seeing reality and analyzing things. Let us leave the real cause to the privacy of the deceased and God.

Many times, wanting to find a reason unconsciously pursues to free us from the feeling of guilt that surrounds us, for not having detected the intention and not having done enough to avoid the action. It will be one of the most difficult obstacles to healing to overcome. This is nothing more than a false accusation, we are not responsible for the suicide of a loved one in any way, shape or form.

"Above all things, love one another intensely,
for love covers an infinity of sins."
(John 4:7-8)

Accept

Being aware of the reality of the facts is an important step. Not avoiding what happened in daily life is key to a speedy recovery.

Particularly for me, when I was asked about my husband, just by not lying about how he died, it helped me to handle the subject in a natural way. I don't know if this is in line with what psychologists suggest, but it worked for me to live in reality, not escape from it.

To everyone who asked me – how did your husband die? – I answered simply: – he committed suicide. You cannot live in a constant lie and telling the truth helps you to face and accept what happened. There is no reason to feel ashamed or afraid of this; there are other worse and really embarrassing things.

If you want to hide the fact, you will isolate yourself from people who do not know what has happened or who find it difficult to talk about it for fear of offending, and perhaps it is in them that you will be able to find the emotional support you need.

As I mentioned before, the loss of a family member is the same event, equally painful, regardless of the events that caused it. Don't allow social norms or fear of what people will say, to slow down or block your family's recovery.

We must be courageous, honest with ourselves and maintain integrity in our answers when faced with questions such as "What happened? Why did you do it?

"Acceptance is not resignation, but nothing wastes more energy than resisting and fighting a situation that you cannot change."
Dalai Lama

※ ※ ※ ※ ※

Duel

Do not repress feelings, handle your grief as it is best for you and not for other people, every human being is different and, therefore, handles things differently.

Cry as many times as you want to cry. My advice is not to do it in front of people, not because of shame or pride, but so that you can cry as you find it emotionally more liberating. Also because not everyone knows how to share a cry, listen and express the right words.

There are many taboos and preconceived ideas on this subject, which said by someone you appreciate could hurt you more and confuse you. Cry in intimacy, talk to God and you will see that the time will come when you will handle your grief with love. Grief is something you will not be able to avoid throughout the process, but you can choose to make the best of it and deal with it in a healthy way.

When one day you wake up and realize that the memories no longer make you suffer so much and that you are even able to speak freely about the virtues of that loved one and not only about the end, you will know that you are beginning to rise up.

*"Blessed are those who mourn, for they shall
be comforted!".*
(Matthew 5:4)

✳ ✳ ✳ ✳ ✳ ✳

Set goals

Find something to do, whatever it is that you like to do, whatever gives you satisfaction, not just work but something extra. I love supporting the rescue of street animals and helping people with different needs. It makes you look around you and realize that there are always people with bigger problems than the ones you face.

Study something new, do crafts, learn a language, do something challenging, the more challenging, the less time there will be to give space to sadness or to encourage negative thoughts.

Setting goals, as many as you want and in the preferred area, will help us to take a big leap in the process, but they must be achievable goals, because it is about starting to give a new meaning to our own life and to move away from a possible depression.

I began to study interior design, something completely different from banking, to which I had always dedicated myself. This apprenticeship, completely unrelated to my professional interests, managed to take me out of the social circle I was used to, to explore other qualities I didn't know I could develop, and it worked successfully for me.

"Strength comes not from bodily capacity, but from the will of the soul."

Mahatma Gandhi

✻ ✻ ✻ ✻ ✻ ✻ ✻

Work out

It has been shown that exercising or any physical activity stimulates endorphins, popularly known as "happiness hormones", which are neurotransmitters in the brain that emit hormones that can make you feel more cheerful, helping to alleviate depression, sadness or pain at the moment you are in.

Physical activity is any activity that works the muscles and requires energy, so it can include some work, household and many recreational tasks.

On the contrary, when we talk about exercising we refer to a planned, structured and repetitive body movement that is performed to improve or maintain physical fitness. If you can't afford a gym, there are now gyms in parks. A good walk or a bike ride, work with the same benefits, -many times better- because they put you in contact with nature and it is proven that nothing is healthier for the spirit than a walk among trees.

Go for a walk, ride a bike or do any physical activity you like, this always helps us to feel better, breathe, relax, sleep better and at the same time keeps us healthy. It is very likely that stress and grief depress your immune system opening a gap for you to get sick more easily.

Physical exercise helps to free your mind from worries so you can get away from negative thoughts that will fuel your depression, anxiety and pain.

I hated the gym, until I started it and began to notice that I slept better, that I felt more energetic. I had to accept that it was a great decision.

"Exercise is key to physical and mental health."
Nelson Mandela

❊ ❊ ❊ ❊ ❊ ❊ ❊

Social interaction

Connect with your friends, especially those who were with you at all times, who accompanied you without question or questioning. Stay away from those who keep asking reckless questions.

Family plays an important role in recovery, give them the opportunity to be with you as you grieve.

Social connection is one of the most powerful factors in combating depression, sadness and grief.

Avoid spending too much time in front of the TV, don't take naps, and visit your friends and family.

If you have the opportunity, make new friends and expand your circle of acquaintances.

"One alone can be defeated, but two can resist.
The three-stranded rope is not easily broken!"
(Ecclesiastes 4:12)

❊ ❊ ❊ ❊ ❊ ❊ ❊ ❊ ❊

Harmonizing with God and connecting with the Holy Spirit

This is undoubtedly the most important thing of all, He will give you the tools to really face anything, He will give you the strength to endure and overcome it.

It was the backbone of my recovery, the security I felt because I had him in my life. It is shocking.

Remember that the Bible repeatedly speaks of God's love for widows and orphans, devoting 76 verses to widows and 40 verses to orphans.

"Father of the fatherless and defender of
widows is God in His holy habitation!"
(Psalm 68:5)

Cling to Him from the depths of your being and He will show you His love.

It is difficult to go against circumstances that we cannot change, but we can open our hearts and use tools that help us adapt to handle the changes and challenges we will face and God will be your best tool.

Grief is the most acute challenge to our trust in God.

"I know that God loves me, and will never forsake me."
(John 3:16; Hebrews 13:5)

"I know that He is for me and not against me."
(Romans 8:31)

"I know that the Word of God is true, and that His heart is kind."
(Psalm 33:4; Acts 14:17)

Reflection

God is a God of love, of forgiveness, and I am sure that he places his hand on the heads of those who immolate themselves to accompany them to their end, especially if they are human beings who have had a worthy trajectory in their journey through life.

It is not an easy journey for those of us who have had to live through such a traumatic experience as the suicide of a family member. It is painful, but love and faith must overcome everything that invades our hearts and minds.

Time is doing its work, we should not rush and live as my parish priest advises "...**one day at a time**".

Every day we should try to create good and beautiful memories with our loved ones, because it is these memories that will help us to face reality, if destiny places us in the situation of losing one of them.

Let us mourn in the way that each of us understands as the best for our own. Let us not allow others to set guidelines in this regard.

Let's love every day as if it were our last, let's express to everyone around us how we feel about them, we don't know when will be the last time we will have the opportunity to say: -I love you- those simple words can make a big difference.

Remember, dear readers, that from the moment you connect with the **Holy Spirit**, all the tools to face, overcome and obtain what you want will be placed in your hands.

No matter what the loss was like, if we could do it, you can do it too. You just have to want to move forward.

God bless you.

"We love Him, because He first loved us.
If anyone says, I love God and hates his
brother, he is a liar. For he who does not love
his brother whom he has seen, how can he love
God whom he has not seen?"
(John 4:19-20)

Epilogue

One day at a time I will live.
One day at a time I will take steps
forward towards what I want to
achieve.
I will take my purpose and I will
accomplish it, with God's help I
will overcome.

One day at a time without fainting,
with constancy and faith that everything is
possible, if I believe.
When I lack the light I will look for it in Jesus,
although I have weaknesses I am strong,
one day at a time.

I will forgive, the past does not distress me
because I decided to free myself from
bitterness, I decide to forgive to free myself
and fly, to untie my ropes of hatred and
rancor.

One day at a time I will triumph,
my steps are affirmed in my beliefs and my courage.
I have no fear,
I go forward, I go with good cheer, one day at a
time.

This edition of Love, Faith and Suicide. A personal experience,
by Flor Del Monte, was completed in November 2021, in the
graphic workshops of Editora Búho, Santo Domingo, Dominican
Republic.